READE

Biography of

Dr. Sarvepalli Radhakrishnan

READER'S DELIGHT

An Imprint of Ramesh Publishing House

NEW DELHI

3rd Edition: February, 2016

ISBN 978-93-5012-254-9

Published by: Alok Kumar Gupta *for* Reader's Delight
(An Imprint of Ramesh Publishing House)

Admin. Office: 12-H, New Daryaganj Road, Opp. Officers' Mess,
New Delhi-110002 ✆ 23261567, 23275224 23275124

Showroom: ● 2604, Balaji Market, Nai Sarak, Delhi-6 ✆ 23253720, 23282525

● 4457, Nai Sarak, Delhi-6 ✆ 23918938

E-Mail: info@rameshpublishinghouse.com
Website: www.rameshpublishinghouse.com

PREFACE

Dr. Sarvepalli Radhakrishnan was an Indian philosopher and statesman. He was the first Vice-president and the second President of India.

He was one of India's most-influential scholars of comparative religion and philosophy. He built a bridge between the East and the West by showing that the philosophical systems of all traditions are comprehensible within the terms of each other. He wrote authoritative exegeses of India's religious and philosophical literature for the English speaking world.

He was the chairman of the University Education Commission. It was under his guidance that the Indian Education system of Independent India was re-framed. Whatever positions he held, he remained a teacher at heart all his life. The teaching profession was his first love and that is why his birthday is still celebrated as 'Teachers' Day' in India.

Among the many honours he received were a knighthood, the Bharat Ratna and the Order of Merit.

The Inside pages contain an interesting account of how a middle class village boy became a great philosopher, educationist and statesman. The book also gives its readers minute detail about his life, career and personality. We hope the book will prove successful in clinching the readers' interest.

—Publisher

Contents

INTRODUCTION

"Spiritual life is the genius of India."

—Dr. S. Radhakrishnan

Dr. Sarvepalli Radhakrishnan was one of the most recognized and influential Indian thinkers in academic circles as an academic, philosopher, and statesman, in the 20th century. Throughout his life and extensive writing career, Radhakrishnan sought to define, defend, and promulgate his religion, a religion he variously identified as Hinduism, Vedanta, and the religion of the Spirit. He sought to demonstrate that his Hinduism was both philosophically coherent and ethically viable. Radhakrishnan's concern for experience and his extensive knowledge of the Western philosophical and literary traditions has earned him the reputation of being a bridge-builder between India and the West. His lengthy writing career and his many published works have been influential in shaping the West's understanding of Hinduism, India, and the East.

He graduated with a Master's Degree in Arts from Madras University. In partial fulfilment for his M.A. degree, Radhakrishnan wrote a thesis on the ethics of the Vedanta titled *"The Ethics of the Vedanta and Its Metaphysical Presuppositions"*, which was a reply to the charge that the Vedanta system had no room for ethics.

He showed how western philosophers, despite all claims to objectivity, were biased by theological influences from their wider culture. In one of his major works, he also showed that Indian philosophy, once translated into standard academic jargon, is worthy of being called philosophy by western standards. His main contribution to Indian thought, therefore, is that he placed it "on the map", thereby earning Indian philosophy a respect that it had not had before.

Dr. Radhakrishnan was of the opinion that only the right kind of education could solve many ills of the society and the country. He wanted to bring in a change in the educational system by improving the quality of education and building up a strong relationship between the teacher and the taught. In his opinion, teachers should be the best minds of the country; they should not merely instruct but should gain the true affection of pupils, and the respect for teachers cannot be ordered but it should be earned.

After 1946, his philosophical career was cut short when India needed him as Ambassador to UNESCO and later to Moscow. He was later to become the first Vice-President and finally the President (1962-1967) of India. He was awarded the Bharat Ratna in 1954. The University of Oxford instituted the Radhakrishnan Chevening Scholarships and the Radhakrishnan Memorial Award in his memory. He also received the Peace Prize of the German Book Trade in 1961.

Even as the President he remained a humble man. It was an open house at the Rashtrapati Bhavan and people from all sections of society were welcome to meet him. In addition, he accepted only ₹ 2,500 out of his salary of ₹ 10,000 and donated the remaining amount to the Prime Minister's National Relief Fund every month. He remained a teacher in many ways and even adopted the authoritative tone of a headmaster in many of his letters to his ministers.

One of the renowned teachers of our century, whose fiery lectures and writings left a lasting impression on audiences around the world, Radhakrishnan regarded education as an instrument to help man to understand and control himself, to relate himself rightly to nature and society, to serve his country and at the same time progress a world outlook.

He envisioned an India built and guided by those who were truly educated and had a personal vision of and commitment to raise Indian self-consciousness.

As President of the Indian Republic, Radhakrishnan acted as friend and Counselor to three Prime Ministers Jawaharlal Nehru, Lal Bahadur Shastri and Indira Gandhi. When Radhakrishnan passed away on 17 April 1975, Indira Gandhi said of him: ..it was our good fortune to have him as Vice-President for ten years and as President for five years. As a Statesman, he had developed understanding of all the practical problems of nation building, and contributed significantly to the consolidation of our political and Parliamentary traditions.

THE FAMILY HISTORY

Sarvepalli Radhakrishnan was born on 5 September 1888 in a poor Telugu Brahmin family at Tiruttani, a town in then Madras Presidency, British India, now in Thiruvallur District, Tamil Nadu, 84 km to the northwest of Madras (now Chennai). His father's name was Sarvepalli Veeraswami and his mother's name was Sitamma. His mother tongue was Telugu. His early years were spent in Tiruttani and Tirupati. His father was a subordinate revenue officer in the service of a local zamindar (landlord). His primary education was at Primary Board High School at Tiruttani. In 1896, he moved to the Hermansburg Evangelical Lutheral Mission School in Tirupati.

His father, it is said, did not want his son to learn English, instead wanted him to become a priest. However, the talents of the boy were so outstanding that he was sent to school at Tirupati and then Vellore.

— ✱✱✱ —

CHILDHOOD & EDUCATION

Sarvepalli Radhakrishnan was born into a middle class Brahman family in south India near Madras (now Chennai). His family valued education, and he attended Christian-sponsored secondary schools and did his higher education at Madras Christian College. During his education, he came to study classical Greek and Western thought, especially Plato, Aristotle and came to know Christian religious views. He  was confronted with Western teachers who held a low opinion of the Hinduism they saw around them and were active in promoting Christian social action, especially in the fields of health, education and poverty reduction.

In 1896, Radhakrishnan was sent to school in the nearby pilgrimage center of Tirupati, a town with a distinctively cosmopolitan flavour, drawing devotees from all parts of India. For four years, he attended the Hermannsburg Evangelical Lutheran Missionary School. It was there that the young Radhakrishnan first encountered non-Hindu missionaries.

Between 1900 and 1904, Radhakrishnan attended Elizabeth Rodman Voorhees College in Vellore, a school run by the American Arcot Mission of the Reformed Church in America.

Christian missionaries, whose, theological emphasis on personal religious experience, suggested to him a common ground between Christianity and his own religious heritage. In Vellore, the presence of a systematic social gospel was intimately bound up with the religion of those who sought to censure Radhakrishnan's cultural norms and religious worldview.

With these experiences informing his worldview that Radhakrishnan encountered a resurgent Hinduism. Specifically, he encountered the writings of Swami Vivekananda and V.D. Savarkar's *The First War of Indian Independence.*

What Vivekananda, Savarkar, and Theosophy did bring to Radhakrishnan was a sense of cultural self-confidence and self-reliance. It was only after his experiences at Madras Christian College that he began to put down in writing his own understanding of Hinduism.

In 1904, Radhakrishnan entered Madras Christian College. At this time his academic sensibilities lay with the physical sciences, and before beginning his MA degree in 1906, his interest appears to have been Law.

Two key influences on Radhakrishnan at Madras Christian College left an indelible stamp on his sensibilities.

It was here that he was trained in European philosophy. He was also introduced to the philosophical methods and theological views of his M.A. supervisor and most influential non-Indian mentor, Professor A.G. Hogg.

Upon the completion of his M.A. degree in 1908, Radhakrishnan found himself at both a financial and professional crossroads. His obligations to his family precluded him from applying for a scholarship to study in Britain and he struggled without success to find work in Madras. The following year, with the assistance of William Skinner at Madras Christian College, he was able to secure what was intended to be a temporary teaching position at Presidency College in Madras.

At Presidency College, Radhakrishnan lectured on a variety of topics in psychology as well as in European philosophy. As a junior Assistant Professor, logic, epistemology and ethical theory were his stock areas of instruction. At the College, he also learned Sanskrit.

MARRIAGE

In 1905 while at Voorhees College, Radhakrishnan married Sivakamamma a distant cousin, at the age of 16. As per tradition the marriage was arranged by the family. They had been married more than fifty years when she died in 1956. They had five daughters and one son. Their son and youngest

Dr. S. Radhakrishnan with Dr. S. Gopal

child, Sarvepalli Gopal, was born on 23 April 1923. A historian and biographer, Dr. Gopal is the author of numerous books on contemporary history in South Asia and the general editor of *Select Works of Jawaharlal Nehru.* Gopal became a Fellow of St. Anthony's College, Oxford in 1966 and has also been Commonwealth Fellow of Trinity College, Cambridge. He was appointed Professor of Contemporary History at Jawaharlal Nehru University, New Delhi in 1972. He has served India in many ways, including as Chairman of the National Book Trust, India (1973-1976).

— *** —

A GREAT CAREER

In April 1909, Sarvepalli
Radhakrishnan was appointed
to the Department of Philosophy at the Madras
Presidency College. There-
after, in 1918, Radhakrishnan
was selected as Professor of
Philosophy by the University
of Mysore. By that time, he
had written many articles for
journals of repute like *The*

Quest, Journal of Philosophy and the *International
Journal of Ethics.* He also completed his first book, *The
Philosophy of Rabindranath Tagore.* He believed Tagore's
philosophy to be the "genuine manifestation of the Indian
spirit". Radhakrishnan's second book, *The Reign of
Religion in Contemporary Philosophy* was published in
1920.

In 1921 he was appointed as a professor in philosophy
to occupy the King George V Chair of Mental and Moral
Science at the University of Calcutta. Radhakrishnan
represented the University of Calcutta at the Congress of

the Universities of the British Empire in June 1926 and the International Congress of Philosophy at Harvard University in September 1926. Another important academic event during this period was the invitation to deliver the Hibbert Lecture on the ideals of life which he delivered at Harris Manchester College, Oxford in 1929 and which was subsequently published in book form as *An Idealist View of Life.*

In 1929, Radhakrishnan was invited to take the post vacated by Principal J. Estlin Carpenter at Harris Manchester College. This gave him the opportunity to lecture to the students of the University of Oxford on Comparative Religion. For his services to education, he was knighted and bestwoed upon the title of 'Sir' by King George V in the June 1931 Birthday Honours, and formally invested with his honour by the Governor-General of India, the Earl of Willingdon, in April 1932. However, he did not use the title in personal life, preferring instead his academic title of 'Doctor'.

He was the Vice-Chancellor of Andhra University from 1931 to 1936. In 1936 Radhakrishnan was named Spalding Professor of Eastern Religions and Ethics at the University of Oxford, and was elected a Fellow of All Souls College. In 1939, Pt. Madan Mohan Malaviya invited him to succeed him as the Vice-Chancellor of Banaras Hindu University (BHU). Radhakrishnan served as its Vice-Chancellor till January 1948.

When India became independent in 1947, Radhakrishnan represented India at UNESCO (1946–52) and was later Ambassador of India to the Soviet Union, from 1949 to 1952. He was also elected to the Constituent Assembly of India.

Radhakrishnan was elected as the first Vice President of India in 1952. He was also elected as the second President of India (1962–1967).

HIS PHILOSOPHY

His first book, *"The Ethics of the Vedanta and Its Material Presupposition"*, being his thesis for the M.A. degree examination of the Madras University, published in 1908, his fame at once established as a great philosopher of undoubted ability. All his later works are landmarks in their respective fields. Expressing abstract and abstruse philosophical thoughts in intelligible language is considered very difficult. But Dr. Radhakrishnan was one of the few who could accomplish this with ease and simplicity.

To him, philosophy was a way of understanding life and his study of Indian philosophy served as a cultural therapy. By interpreting Indian thought in western terms and showing that it was imbued with reason and logic he was able to give Indians a new sense of esteem, who were overcome by inferiority complex by imperial forces. But he also made clear to them that their long and rich tradition had been arrested and required further evolution and he exhorted Indians to cast off much that was corrupt and abhorrent.

— ✱✱✱ —

HIS SOCIAL COMMITMENT

Dr. Radhakrishnan moved beyond being a mere academic and sought to engage his philosophical and religious studies in the political and social developments of the contemporary context.

Dr. Sarvepalli Radhakrishnan with Rabindra Nath Tagore.

He believed that in India, the philosopher's duty was to keep in touch with the past while stretching out to the future. This commitment to society, the crusading urgent tone in his scholarly writings, the modern note in his interpretations of even classical texts and his intellectual resistance to the deforming pressures of colonialism gave Dr. Radhakrishnan a distinct public image. He was a coin minted differently from the usual run of politicians and academicians.

— ✱✱✱ —

18

AN EVOCATIVE TEACHER

Far from being a stern and severe intellectual remote from the world, Dr. Radhakrishnan was a very humane person. Exceedingly popular among his students right from his early days as a professor at Presidency College, Madras he was an evocative teacher. He was offered the professorship in Calcutta University when he  was less than 30 years old. He served as Vice-Chancellor of Andhra University from 1931 to 1936. In 1939, he was appointed the Vice Chancellor of Banaras Hindu University. Two years later, he took over the Sir Sayaji Rao Chair of Indian Culture and Civilisation in Banaras.

Recognition of his scholarship came again in 1936, when he was invited to fill the Chair of Spalding Professor of Eastern Religions and Ethics at Oxford which he retained for 16 years. His mastery on his subject and his clarity of thought and expression made him a much sought after teacher. But what made him even more popular was his warm-heartedness and his ability to draw out people. This aspect of his personality continued to win him countless admirers throughout his long and illustrious public life.

In the last decades of British rule, his was the most sophisticated and exalted analysis of Gandhi's work and thought and in free India he provided the ideological armour for Nehru's foreign policy.

DR. RADHAKRISHNAN & POLITICS

One of the personality traits of Radhakrishnan was his great aptitude for politics, which was noticeable by the time he was in his late forties. It was observed that if Radhakrishnan cared to enter politics, he would become one of the biggest men of the epoch, because he was the only man of his generation capable of providing Indian nationalism with a creed, a theory, reconciling India's immemorial intellectual tradition with the demands of a changing social order. It was also observed that though several of his friends urged him to enter politics, he put them off, saying that he was very much content with his work and the fellowship of his friends. In 1936, the British head of the education system of the Madras presidency prophesied that if and when India became a republic, Radhakrishnan would become its president.

In the late forties he was forcasted possible imminent entry into politics as well as his very probable success in it, because he was so well-equipped for it. This was indeed so, because by then Radhakrishnan had enough independent income of his own; he had ingratiated himself with the most important national leaders; and, above all, through his writings and speeches he had by the late

1940s established himself as a forceful and fearless advocate of independence for India. Radhakrishnan is described as an academic revolutionary.

The issues of education and nationalism come together for Radhakrishnan during this period. For Radhakrishnan, a university education which quickened the development of the whole individual was the only responsible and practical means to the creation of Indian solidarity and clarity of national vision. Throughout the 1930s and 1940s, Radhakrishnan expressed his vision of an autonomous India. He envisioned an India built and guided by those who were truly educated, by those who had a personal vision of and commitment to raising Indian self-consciousness.

Radhakrishnan, never participated in the struggle for independence and never went to prison. Rather he contributed to India through his education, knowledge and philosophy. He was knighted by the King-emperor in 1931; and invited to be a professor at Oxford in 1936 and a fellow of the British Academy in 1939. At home, the Mysore government under the distinguished Diwan Visvesvarayya appointed him a professor in their newly established university in 1916, but Ashutosh Mookerjee snatched him away to Calcutta in 1921. He was elected Vice-Chancellor of Andhra University in 1931, while Pandit Madan Mohan Malaviya got him elected as Vice-Chancellor of Banaras Hindu University in 1939. When India became free, he became member of the Constituent Assembly,

Ambassador to the USSR, the Vice-President for two terms, and finally, the President. He relinquished his Knighthood in 1947, after India became free.

When compared to Mahatma Gandhi, Subhash Chandra Bose, Jawaharlal Nehru or Sardar Patel, he may be said to have done nothing substantial directly for the independence of India. But without making a frontal attack on political problems, he attempted to convince the English-knowing world that India with its great culture and high intellectual tradition, extending back to centuries, cannot and should not remain a subject nation and that it was not moral for Britain to continue its domination. No Indian academic with a world-wide reputation advocated complete independence for India so eloquently, forcibly and frequently in as open a manner and for so long a time as Radhakrishnan did at home and abroad.

From the 1920s till he had a stroke in 1968, in every available form he asserted the equality of East and West, urged that imperialism and colonialism be ended, and pleaded for the replacement of existing world politico-economic order by a new one based on social and economic justice. It was to Jawaharlal Nehru's credit that he perceived the advantage to the nation of having a man like Dr. Radhakrishnan as its Ambassador, Vice-President and, finally President.

— *** —

HIS INTERNATIONAL ACCLAIM

His commitment to high principles and unfailing dignity lent nobility and moral authority to all the offices which he held. If in India Dr. Radhakrishnan was a highly respected

Dr. S. Radhakrishnan with Queen Elizabeth & Dr. Rajendra Prasad

figure, abroad he became one of the best-liked public figures of his time. He earned very early international recognition as a philosopher. In 1952, the Library of Living Philosophers, an institute of world-wide repute, brought out a massive volume on *'The Philosophy of Sarvepalli Radhakrishnan'* devoted wholly to a critical appreciation of his philosophical doctrines.

After Independence, this philosophical luminary, who personified the essence of India yet had a universal vision, became an ideal ambassador to the Soviet Union, for the nascent nation poised to establish itself in the international arena.

— ✱✱✱ —

PRESIDENT OF THE NATION

In 1952, Dr. Radhakrishnan was chosen to be the Vice-President of the Republic of India and in 1962, he became the President of India for five years. It was the glory of Indian democracy that an

Dr. S. Radhakrishnan, accompanied by Vice-President Dr. Zakir Hussain

educationist aloof from politics but with an international acclaim as a profound scholar was placed in the position of the President. And it was an advantage for a young country like India to have him to interpret its domestic and foreign policies abroad to expound its outlook and aspirations emphatically and in the right way which was much needed in a world of uncertainty and disbelief among other nations.

His appointment as President was hailed by Bertrand Russel who said "It is an honour to philosophy that Dr. Radhakrishnan should be President of India and I, as a philosopher, take special pleasure in this. Plato aspired for philosophers to become kings and it is a tribute to India that she should make a philosopher her President".

History reserved, for Radhakrishnan's term of office as President, much suspense and surprise. Within months of his ascendancy in 1962, there was the Chinese invasion. The nation's morale was dealt a blow but Radhakrishnan's voice, firm and resolute came on the air to reassure a shaken nation:

"Owing to the difficult terrain and numerical superiority of the Chinese, we suffered military reverses. These have opened our eyes to the realities of the situation. We are now aware of our inadequacies and are alive to the needs of the present and the demands of the

Dr. S. Radhakrishnan with Indian Army officers during the clash with China.

future. The country has developed a new purpose, a new will".

In 1965, Pakistan violated our Western frontiers. Dr. Radhakrishnan in his broadcast to the nation on September 25, 1965 said, "Pakistan assumed that India was too weak or too afraid or too proud to fight. India, though naturally disinclined to take to arms, felt the necessity to defend herself when attacked. Pakistan also assumed that communal disturbances would occur in the country and in the resulting chaos she could have her way. Her miscalculations must have come to her as a rude shock."

Dr. Radhakrishnan had great faith in Indian democracy. In his farewell broadcast to the Nation on May 12, 1967, he said, "Despite occasional forebodings to the contrary," the Indian Constitution has worked successfully so far. "But democracy", he warned, "was more than a system of the Government". "It was a way of life and a regime of civilised conduct of human affairs. We should be the architects of peaceful changes and the advocates of radical reform", he said.

ORIGIN OF TEACHERS' DAY

It was in 1962, when Dr. Radhakrishnan became the President of India that his birthday in September came to be observed as 'Teachers' Day'. It is a tribute to Dr. Radhakrishnan's close association with the cause of teachers. Whatever position he held whether as President or Vice-President or even as Ambassador, Dr.  Radhakrishnan essentially remained a teacher throughout his life. The teaching profession was his first love and those who studied under him still remember with gratitude his great qualities as a teacher. Dr. Sarvepalli Radhakhrishnan was a philosopher and a teacher par excellence.

Since 1962, 5th of September has been celebrated as Teachers' Day in India. On his first-birthday after becoming the president of India some of his students and friends approached him and requested him to allow them to celebrate his birthday. In reply, Dr. Radhakrishnan said,

"Instead of celebrating my birthday separately, it would be my proud privilege if September 5th is observed as Teachers' day". This shows Dr. Radhakrishnan's love for the teaching profession and clearly indicates that he considered a teacher in him, and in everyone, above the honour of even the President of India. From then onwards, his birthday is observed as Teachers' Day in India.

Pandit Jawaharlal Nehru, who was one of his closest friends throughout, said about Dr. Radhakrishnan, "He has served his country in many capacities but above all, he is a great teacher from whom all of us have learnt much and will continue to learn. It is India's peculiar privilege to have a great philosopher, a great educationist and a great humanist as her President. That in itself shows the kind of men we honour and respect."

SOME MAJOR EVENTS

While at Madras Christian Missionary College, young Radhakrishnan was undecided about the choice of subject for his honours course. He was expected to choose from Mathematics, Physics, Biology, History and Philosophy. It was a mere incidence that one of his cousin who had completed his graduation course with honours in Philosophy, passed on to him three well known books on Philosophy. Radhakrishnan read those books mere out of curiosity and finally decided to opt for Philosophy as an honours course at graduation level.

In 1914, the world renowned Mathematics genius from India, Srinivasan Ramanujan visited Sarvepalli Radhakrishnan to seek his blessings before leaving for his studies in Cambridge. He approached him with the message that Goddess Durga had directed him in his dream to seek his blessings before leaving India.

Ashutosh Mookerjee, the Vice-Chancellor of Calcutta University was highly impressed by the articles and books of Sarvepalli Radhakrishnan. He nominated him to the post of King George V Professor of Philosophy at Calcutta University in 1921. It was a highly prestigious assignment.

Prof. J.H. Murihead requested Sarvepalli Radha-krishnan to write a readable account on Indian Philosophy which could be included in the Library of Philosophy. Radhakrishnan completed a mammoth task of writing on Indian religion within two years and published the book *"Indian Philosophy"* in two volumes in the year 1923. The book is still rated as "philosophical classic and a literary masterpiece".

Sarvepalli Radhakrishnan was invited to Oxford University to deliver "Upton Lecture" on 'The Hindu View of Life'. Later a special chair was established for him and he was appointed as Spalding Professor of East Religion and Ethics at Oxford.

In 1929, Sarvepalli Radhakrishnan succeeded Principal J. Estin Carpenter in Manchester College, Oxford.

He was knighted in 1931 and bestowed upon the title of 'Sir'. He was then called Sir S. Radhakrishnan. He was called by that title till 1947. After that he was addressed as Dr. S. Radhakrishnan.

In 1931, he was invited to head the Andhra University as Vice-Chancellor. He resurrected the university by restructuring the departments of Language, Humanities, Science and Technology. When he left the university in 1936, Andhra University had earned the position of the leading universities of India.

In 1939, he took over as the Vice-Chancellor of Banaras Hindu University. The Governor Sir Maurice Hallet tried to convert the campus of University into a war hospital during the Quit India Movement. Radhakrishnan approached the Viceroy and got stayed the conversion of campus for other purposes. However, Sir Maurice Hallet responded by holding back the grant to the University. Then Dr. Sarvepalli Radhakrishnan launched a 'Begging Pilgrimage' and collected funds for the university. The university continued to work in that manner.

Dr. S. Radhakrishnan with Yugoslav Leader Tito.

Sarvepalli Radhakrishnan was appointed as an Ambassador to USSR in 1949. He was invited by Joseph Stalin to meet him in Kremlin. When Radhakrishnan was called back to India in 1952, he met Stalin before leaving and had very intimate conversation with Stalin. It touched Stalin deeply and he, wished him a long life.

During his two terms as Vice-President of India, whereby he acted as the Chairman of Rajya Sabha, his period is remembered for tactful handling of sensitive debates in Rajya Sabha.

— ✱✱✱ —

COMMENTS & QUOTATIONS

Dr. Sarvepalli Radha-krishnan was a monist in philosophy, monotheist in religion, eudaemonist or perfectionist in Ethics and socialist in politics.

JFK & Dr. Sarvepalli Radhakrishnan, 3 Jun 1963.

Professor A. G. Hogg of Madras Missionary College while commen-ding the post graduate thesis of Sarvepalli Radhakrishnan titled "The Ethics of Vedanta and Its Metaphysical Presupposition" wrote, "The thesis which he prepared in the second year of his study for this degree shows a remarkable understanding of the main aspects of the philosophical problems, a capacity for handling easily a complex argument besides more than the average mastery of good English".

In Dr. Radhakrishnan's own words, "Religious feeling must establish itself as a rational way of living. If ever the spirit is to be at home in this world, and not merely a prisoner or a fugitive, spiritual foundations must be laid deep and preserved worthily. Religion must express itself in reasonable thought, fruitful action and right social institutions."

In 1929, Radhakrishnan was invited to take the post vacated by Principal J. Estin Carpenter in Manchester College, Oxford. This gave him the opportunity to lecture to the students of University of Oxford on Comparative Religion. During that visit, he also gave the Hibbert Lectures on "An Idealist View of Life" to audiences at the Universities of London and Manchester. In his own words, "It was a great experience for me to preach from Christian pulpits in Oxford and Birmingham, in Manchester and Liverpool. It heartened me to know that my addresses were liked by Christian audiences. Referring to my sermon on "Revolution through Suffering", an Oxford daily observed, "Though the Indian preacher had the marvellous power to weave a magic web of thought, imagination and language, the real greatness of his sermon resides in some indefinable spiritual quality which arrests attention, moves the heart and lifts us into an ampler air."

Aldous Huxley had remarked about Radhakrishnan, "He is the master of words and no words". It refers to his ability to express the most abstruse thoughts of philosophy in such a fine language that it becomes comprehensible to all.

Prof. H.N. Muirhead said, "Dr. Radhakrishnan has the rare qualification of being equally versed in the great European and the not less great Asiatic tradition which may be said to hold in solution between them the spiritual wisdom of the world, and of thus speaking as a philosophical bilinguist upon it."

George P. Conger said, "Among the philosophers of our time, no one has achieved so much in so many fields as has Sarvepalli Radhakrishnan of India."

Further, "With his unique appointment at Banaras and Oxford, like a weaver's shuttle, he has gone to and fro between the East and West, carrying a thread of understanding, weaving it into the fabric of civilization."

Another profound scholar and leading politician Dr. Shanker Dayal Sharma, when took over as the President of India, it was popular in intellectual circle, "A person that could revive the glory of President of India as raised to a height by Dr. S. Radhakrishnan, had come become president."

SOME EXCERPTS FROM SPEECHES

Some excerpts from speeches of Dr. S. Radhakrishnan are:

"If we claim to be civilized, if we love justice, if we cherish mercy, if we are not ashamed to own the reality of the inward light, we must affirm that we are first and foremost Citizens of the World...Our planet has grown too small for parochial patriotism."

"The present crisis in human affairs is due to a profound crisis in human consciousness, a lapse from the organic wholeness of life. Today, there is a crisis of perception, a widespread sense of unease concerning old forms of thinking which require that we must recreate and re-enact a vision of the world based on the elements of reverence, order, and human dignity, without which no society can be held together."

"If we are to help the present society to grow organically into a world order, we must make it depend on the universal and enduring values which are implanted in the human heart that each individual is sacred, that we are born for love and not hat. We have learned to live peacefully in larger and larger units. The concept of a community has grown from a narrow tribal basis to the

Nation State. There is no stopping short of a world community. Thus we rejoice that there is an institution like the United Nations, for it is the symbol and

Dr. Radhakrishnan and Dr. Zakir Hussain with students.

hope of the new world, of the light dawning beyond the clouds, clouds piled up by our past patterns of behaviour, past ways of speaking, judging and acting, which do not answer to the deep desire of the peoples of the world for peace and progress. We owe it to ourselves to find out why the light does not spread and disperse the darkness, why the sky is still clouded by fear and suspicion, hate and bitterness."

"If an ancient Indian of the time of the Upanishads, of the Buddha, or the later classical age were to be set down in modern India, he would see his race clinging to forms and shells and rags of the past and missing nine-tenths of its nobler meaning…he would be amazed by the extent of the mental poverty, the immobility, the static repetition, the cessation of science, the long sterility of art, the comparative feebleness of the creative intuition."

"Stagnant systems, like pools, breed obnoxious growths, while flowing rivers constantly renew their waters from fresh springs of inspiration. There is nothing wrong in absorbing the culture of other peoples; only we must enhance, raise and purify the elements we take over, fuse them with the best in our own. Indian philosophy acquires a meaning and a justification for the present only if it advances and ennobles life."

"If we are to shape a community of spirit among the people of the world which is essential for a truly human society and lasting peace, we must forge bonds of international understanding. This can be achieved by an acquaintance with the masterpieces of literature, art and science produced in different countries. When we are in contact with them, we are lifted from the present and immediate passions and interests and move on the mountain tops where we breath a larger air. For out of the anguish of our times is being born a new unity of all mankind in which the free spirit of man can find peace and safety. It is in our power to end the fears which afflict humanity, and save the world from the disaster that impends. Only we should be men of a universal cast of mind, capable of interpreting peoples to one another and developing faith that is the only antidote to fear. The threat to our civilization can be met only on the deeper levels of consciousness. If we fail to overcome the discord between power and spirit, we will be destroyed by the forces which we had the knowledge to create but not the wisdom to control."

Dr. Radhakrishnan used his lectures as a platform to further India's cause for freedom. He thundered, "India is not a subject to be administered but a nation seeking its soul." He would graphically describe the "shame of subjection and the lines of sorrow" apparent on every Indian face.

Dr. S. RADHAKRISHNAN
IN DIFFERENT PERSPECTIVES

An Integral View

Dr. Sarvepalli Radhakrishnan had an integral view of the individual society and the world community. This integral view was like a thread that ran through and held together his philosophy of education, of religion and social regeneration, and of the One World of the human family. He perceived the building of this One World as the challenge to statesmanship in the era after the Second World War and the advent of nuclear weaponry.

Pursuit of Philosophy

Similarly, the pursuit of philosophy meant to Radhakrishnan not only a supreme intellectual effort in search of synthesis but also an attempt to restore order and values to individual and collective human activity. He believed in the creation of a new outlook and a new way of life which will establish the fundamental unity of man's life on Earth.

The World-Man

During his long and distinguished association with UNESCO, Radhakrishnan always emphasized the basic unity of all religions, the common factors between the philosophies of the East and the West, and the need to build up "a world brain, a world mind or a world culture". The major project on mutual appreciation of Eastern and Western cultural values which UNESCO initiated in 1956, owed a great deal to his inspiration.

Mohammed Rafi with President Dr. Sarvepalli Radhakrishnan.

A Great Synthesiser

Radhakrishnan had the great gift of being able to reconcile and synthesise seemingly different, if not contrary view points and values. His genius as a synthesiser found expression in numerous ways.

He fused the concept, inspired by religion, of a humane and equitable social order with the modern concept of socialism. Gandhiji, employing traditional cultural idiom, spoke of the ideal state as *Rama Rajya* and called for the service of *Daridranarayana* or God in the form of the poor and the deprived. He envisaged, "An India in which there shall be no high class and low class of people, an India in which all communities shall live in perfect harmony. There can be no room in such an India for the course of untouchability. Women will enjoy the same rights as men. This is the India of my dreams".

The India envisioned by Gandhiji, in a sense, what could be described, in non-religious terms, as a secular, democratic and socialist republic. No wonder that Radhakrishnan said "The Socialist implications of freedom were understood by Gandhi, we should work for social and national integration, emancipation of women, and absolute social equality, complete abolition of untouchability and caste discrimination, and removal of economic disparities". Radhakrishnan's own belief in the possibility and necessity of a peaceful but fundamental change is summed up in his memorable affirmation "We should be the advocates of peaceful change and advocates of radical reforms".

Views on Secularism

Radhakrishnan did not see a conflict between, and was able to reconcile, secularism and a genuinely religious inclination. He was Chairman of the first University Education Commission, whose report pointed out that, under the Constitution, "There is no state religion. All the different forms are given equal place, provided they do not lead to corrupt practices. Each one is at liberty to approach the unseen as it suits his capacity and inclination. If this is the basis of our secular state, to be secular is not to be religiously illiterate. It is to be deeply spiritual and not narrowly religious". The Commission accordingly recommended that the profoundly humanist insights of all the major religions of the World should be taught at every stage of education.

Planning and Liberty

Similarly, Radhakrishnan saw no conflict between economic planning and individual liberty. He said, "We have to provide ourselves with the material conditions of life—food, clothing and shelter before we can develop—we believe in control, planning and regulation. So far as the art of living is concerned—Literature, Philosophy, Religion, Meditation and Worship—we believe in absolute freedom".

An Astute Analyst

Radhakrishnan's great success in his role as statesman is attributable to his gift of a synthesizing insight. Those who knew of Radhakrishnan only as a Philosopher were somewhat surprised when he was invited by Jawaharlal Nehru in 1949 to serve as India's Ambassador to Moscow in history and current affairs, of which he was an astute analyst. Nehru described Radhakrishnan as "the symbol of India" and said "It is a matter of satisfaction to me that at this very difficult post we have a man of ability, who has a capacity to understand and make others understand also".

A Successful Ambassador

The Soviet Union was at that time inclined to be dogmatic and to regard India as having become only nominally independent. Radhakrishnan's tenure as Ambassador in Moscow saw not only the clearing of the mists of misunderstanding but the laying of the foundation of co-operation between the two countries in the economic and political spheres. The progress of this co-operation over two decades was to culminate in the Indo-Soviet Treaty of Peace, Friendship and Co-operation that was signed in 1971.

A Man of Eminence

The eminent position of Radha-krishnan as an elder statesman was recognized when, within weeks of his return from the assignment in Moscow, he was elected in 1952, unopposed as Vice-President of the Republic. In this capacity he presided over the Rajya Sabha as its Chairman with great distinction.

Dr. S. Radhakrishnan with Dr Rajendra Prasad.

As President

When Radhakrishnan was elected as President of the Republic, Jawaharlal Nehru said on the floor of the Rajya Sabha on May 11, 1962 "Today is the last day when we shall have the honour of your presiding over this House. Henceforth you will preside over an even more important organization, that is, nation itself. We are a little sad that you are leaving us, because you have made this a rather unique place and converted it into a family, sometimes apparently quarreling but really a family, under your guidance.

On the other hand, you will exercise your charm to convert this huge nation also into a large family what we call national integration".

A Keen President

More than any other President or Vice-President, Radhakrishnan took a keen interest in the country's foreign policy. Both during the ten years of his Vice-Presidency and as President, he undertook numerous visits abroad at the instance of Jawaharlal Nehru. Whereever he went, Radhakrishnan was heard with attention and respect because of his intellectual and moral stature and his humane approach to persons and problems. He endeavoured to consolidate and strengthen India's external relations and to bring the United States of America and the Soviet Union to a better understanding of each other.

During these visits, as well as in his talks with the leaders of other countries when they came to India, Radhakrishnan would express his views with friendliness and candour. He did not hesitate to interpret India's Socialist aspirations to American audiences, or to commend intellectual and creative freedom to the leaders of the Soviet Union.

At U.S. Senate

Addressing the United States senate on November 17, 1954, Radhakrishnan said, "We realize that political freedom is not an end itself. It is a means to social equality and economic justice". He reminded his listeners of what

Thomas Jefferson had said in the last letter he ever wrote, "The mass of mankind was not born with saddles on their backs, nor a favoured few booted and spurred, ready to ride them legitimately by the grace of God".

Radhakrishnan went on to say, "We, in our country, are now engaged in the enterprise of affecting a social and economic revolution. The word "revolution" need not scare us. It does not mean barricades and bloodshed. It means only speedy and drastic changes".

On Soviet-Union

Similarly, while responding to the speeches of the Soviet leaders Marshal Bulganin and Nikita Khrushchev at an informal meeting with members of the Indian Parliament on November 31, 1955 Radhakrishnan said, "Now that the Soviet Union has consolidated its base and provided its people with the vital things of life without which they cannot live, we hope they will give them opportunities to develop the grace of the mind and the virtues of the spirit without which life is not worth living".

Again, on a visit to the Soviet Union in September 1964, Radhakrishnan said in the course of a speech on Moscow Television, "The Soviet Union in recent times is placing great emphasis on intellectual, artistic and spiritual values. Freedom of thought is the nerve centre, so to say, of every kind of higher life, intellectual and artistic. And as I look around I find a greater intellectual freedom, greater intellectual co-operation, greater cultural unification taking place in the Soviet Union and in other countries also. We must make the World safe for diversity, for peace, for cultural co-operation, for international understanding".

Views on Co-existance

Sarvepalli Radhakrishnan constantly stressed that the peaceful co-existence commended by India was "not a policy of passive and negative co-existence but one of active and fruitful co-operation among the people of the world". Again he said, "when we talk about co-existence, it does not mean that the aggrieved and the aggressor should live together. We will do our utmost to help the oppressed to redeem themselves from oppression".

Association with Nehru

Radhakrishnan's longest and closest association in public life was with Jawaharlal Nehru. The relationship between the two calls for mutual under-standing and respect, candour and trust. These prevailed in the highest degree during the years that Radhakrishnan was President and Jawaharlal Nehru was Prime Minister.

There was a void in Radhakrishnan's life, as in that of the country, with the death of Jawaharlal Nehru in May

1964. In a broadcast to the nation, Dr. Radhakrishnan described Nehru as "an earnest of the age to come, the age of the world men with world compassion. The best way to honour his memory is to get on with the work which he left unfinished, his work for peace, justice and freedom at home and abroad".

 — ✱✱✱ —

THE LAST TRIBUTE

Dr. Sarvepalli Radhakrishnan died of heart failure in a Madras nursing home on 17 April 1975 after a prolonged illness. He was cremated the same day with full state honours. After elaborate Hindu rites, his son, Dr. Sarvepalli Gopal, lighted the funeral pyre. Radhakrishnan was a vegetarian, non-smoker, and teetotaler. Reading was his favourite leisure activity. He enjoyed cricket, often joining his grandchildren in a game. His memberships, awards, and honours would make a very long list and he would probably be the first one to pass over such a list, anyway.

He received honorary degrees from the University of London, Oxford University, Cambridge University, and more than fifty other universities. A famous teacher of philosophy, educational leader, and statesman is dead. But an equally famous scholar is alive and well both in his writings which continue to attract well-deserved attention and in his speeches which echo in the memories of those fortunate enough to have heard him speak.

Dr. S. Radhakrishanan spent his last days at his house 'Girija' Mylapore, Chennai.

— *** —

AWARDS & HONOURS

Dr Radhakrishnan was appointed a Knight Bachelor in 1931. He was elected Fellow of the British Academy in 1938. He was awarded the Bharat Ratna in 1954 and the Order of Merit in 1963. He received the Peace Prize of the German Book Trade in 1961 and the Templeton Prize in 1975, a few months before his death. He donated the entire amount of the Templeton Prize to Oxford University.

In 1989, Oxford University instituted the Radhakrishnan Scholarships in his memory. The scholarships were later renamed the "Radhakrishnan Chevening Scholarships".

More than 100 honorary degrees and nearly 10 D. Litt had been conferred upon him.

Radhakrishnan was nominated for the Nobel Prize for Literature for five consecutive years from 1933–1937, although he did not win. His nominator was Hjalmar Hammarskjöld, father of Dag Hammarskjöld.

— ✳✳✳ —

BOOKS & WORKS BY DR. S. RADHAKRISHNAN

- Indian Philosophy (1923) Vol.1,738 pages. Vol 2, 807 pages. Oxford University Press.

- The Hindu View of Life (1926), 92 pages

- An Idealist View of Life (1929), 351 pages

- Review: E.A. Burtt (Cornell University), The Philosophical Review, Vol. 44, No. 2, (Mar., 1935), pp. 205–207

- Eastern Religions and Western Thought (1939), Oxford University Press, 396 pages

- Religion and Society (1947), George Allen and Unwin Ltd., London, 242 pages

- The Bhagavadgita with an introductory essay, Sanskrit text, English translation and notes (1948), 388 pages

- The Dhammapada (1950), 194 pages, Oxford University Press

- The Principal Upanishads (1953), 958 pages, Harper Collins Publishers Limited

- Recovery of Faith (1956), 205 pages
- A Source Book in Indian Philosophy (1957), 683 pages, Princeton University Press
- Review: E.A. Burtt (Cornell University), The Philosophical Review, Vol. 67, No. 3, (July 1958), pp. 411–412
- Religion, Science & Culture (1968), 121 pages.

— ✱✱✱ —

CHRONOLOGY OF EVENTS

5th September, 1888	Birth of S. Radhakrishnan
1896	Attended School at Tirupati
1904	Married
1904-1908	Attented Madras Christian College
1909	Lecturership at Presidency College, Madras
1914	Met S. Ramanujan, Mathemetician
1920	Became Professor of Philosophy at University of Mysore
1921	Took up George V Chair at Calcutta University
1926	Invited to Oxford for Lecture
1931	Knighted
1931	Appointed Vice-Chancellor of Andhra University
1933-37	Nominated five times for Nobel Prize for Literature
1938	Elected Fellow of the British Academy

1939	Appointed Vice-Chancellor of Banaras Hindu University
1948	Chaired the University Education Commission
1949	Appointed Ambassador to USSR
5th April 1952	Met Stalin in Kremlin
1952	Elected Vice-President of India
1954	Conferred Bharat Ratna
1956	Wife Passed Away
1961	Received Peace Prize of German Book Trade
1962	Elected President of India
1962	Indo-China War
1963	Conferred Order of Merit
27th May 1964	Jawaharlal Nehru's death
1965	Indo-Pak war won
1967	Completed Presidential Term
1975	Received Templeton Prize
17th April, 1975	Expired

— ✳✳✳ —

SOME RARE PHOTOGRAPHS

06 October 1956, Tokyo, Japan. Dr. Sarvepalli Radhakrishnan, with Japanese empress Nagako, Crown Prince Aikhito (Standing) and emperor Hirohito.

King George, and President of Yugoslavia Marshal Tito, Dr. S Radhakrishnan, during Josip's visit to Gwalior.

President of India Dr Rajendra Prasad felicitates Dr. S. Radhakrishnan,
Vice President of India (left) with Bharat Ratna, at Rashtrapati Bhawan in
New Delhi on January 31, 1955.

Dr. Sarvepalli Radhakrishnan at New Delhi in 1960.

CPSIA information can be obtained
at www.ICGtesting.com
Printed in the USA
LVHW050955050321
680568LV00017B/527